"Sit down and read. Educate yourself for the coming conflicts."

"I am not unaware that leaders betray, and sell out, and play false."

"You must stand for free speech in the streets."

"The future is in labor's strong, rough hands."

"And who is responsible for this appalling child slavery? Everyone!"

"No matter what your fight, don't be ladylike!"

"Not all the coal that is dug warms the world."

"My address is like my shoes: it travels with me.... I abide where there is a fight against wrong."

For Mother Schwartz, as fierce a promoter of social justice

as you'll find in the children's book world —J.W.

For my aunt Caryl, who is changing the world one vote at a time —N.C.

A Note on the Quotes Used in the Story

The author was so inspired by Mother Jones's speeches that he chose to use her as the narrator of her own story. The last two quotes in all capital letters are excerpts from speeches Mother Jones actually gave during her Children's Crusade. She also said, "I will tell the truth wherever I please," one of her most oft-quoted phrases, and "outside the birds sang and the blue sky shone," which was taken from her autobiography.

The illustrated quotes on the endpapers showcase favorite sayings of Mother Jones. "No matter what your fight, don't be ladylike!" and "You must stand for free speech in the streets" come from a speech she gave in 1914 in front of Cooper Union in New York City to a group of five hundred women. In 1910, Mother Jones was asked where she lived by a member of Congress, to which she replied: "My address is like my shoes: it travels with me. . . . I abide where there is a fight against wrong." Mother Jones is said to have often encouraged miners and strikers with the words "Sit down and read. Educate yourself for the coming conflicts." All other quotes—"Not all the coal that is dug warms the world," "And who is responsible for this appalling child slavery? Everyone," "I am not unaware that leaders betray, and sell out, and play false," and "The future is in labor's strong, rough hands"—were taken from her autobiography.

Text copyright © 2020 by Jonah Winter • Jacket art and interior illustrations copyright © 2020 by Nancy Carpenter • All rights reserved. Published in the United States by Schwartz & Wade Books, an imprint of Random House Children's Books, a division of Penguin Random House LLC, New York. • Schwartz & Wade Books and the colophon are trademarks of Penguin Random House LLC. • Photo credits, page 37: top left, "'Mother' Jones and a Group of Girl Strikers" from *The Comrade: An Illustrated Socialist Monthly*, Vol. 2, No. 11, Aug. 1903, pg. 253, housed at the Library of Princeton University; top right, Library of Congress, LC-B2-3049-6 [P&P]; bottom left, Library of Congress, LC-DIG-ds-07713 [P&P]; bottom right, Library of Congress, LC-B2-3354-10 [P&P]. • Visit us on the Web! rhcbooks.com • Educators and librarians, for a variety of teaching tools, visit us at RHTeachersLibrarians.com • *Library of Congress Cataloging-in-Publication Data* • Names: Winter, Jonah, author. | Carpenter, Nancy, illustrator. • Title: Mother Jones and her army of Mill Children / Jonah Winter; Nancy Carpenter, [illustrator]. Description: New York City: Schwartz & Wade, [2020] | Audience: Age: 4–8. | Audience: K to Grade 3. • Identifiers: LCCN 2018052474| ISBN 978-0-449-81291-4 (hardcover) ISBN 978-0-449-81292-1 (hardcover library binding) | ISBN 978-0-449-81293-8 (ebook) • Subjects: LCSH: Jones, Mother, 1837–1930. | Women labor leaders—United States—Biography—Juvenile literature. Labor movement—United States—History—Juvenile literature. • Classification: LCC HD8073.J6 W56 2020 | DDC 331.88092 [B]—dc23 • The text of this book is set in 14-point Brandon Grotesque.The illustrations were rendered in watercolor and digitally. • MANUFACTURED IN CHINA 10 9 8 7 6 5 4 3 2 1 • First Edition • Random House Children's Books supports the First Amendment and celebrates the right to read.

MOTHER JONES
AND HER ARMY OF MILL CHILDREN

words by
Jonah Winter

illustrations by
Nancy Carpenter

schwartz & wade books • new york

My name is Mother Jones,

and I'm MAD.

And **you'd** be MAD, too, if you'd
seen what I've seen.

I've seen coal miners in West Virginia, covered with soot, lungs filled with dust, hardly being paid DIDDLY-SQUAT,

while over yonder the mine owners sit inside their mansions sippin' tea, pettin' their poodles, and gettin' RICHER off the SWEAT of the coal miners.

I've seen factory workers gettin' SHOT AT by company guards, just for takin' part in protests demanding decent pay for their hard, HARD work.

And I've seen the inside of a jail cell, just because I STOOD UP and SPOKE OUT for *the workers of the world—my children*!

"Trespassing" is always the charge—on account of the fact I'll just march right into a factory and speak my mind. "Trespassing"—HA! I will TELL THE TRUTH **wherever** I please. I'm what's called an AGITATOR. I tell the truth about the wretched conditions for workers—and get folks RILED UP.

Well, I've seen lots of things to get RILED UP about, but the worst thing I *ever* saw was in the fabric mills of Philadelphia. I saw children YOUR AGE—nine and ten years old—who worked like grown-ups, forced to stand on their feet for TEN HOURS STRAIGHT,

tying threads to spinning spools, reaching their hands inside the dangerous machines that make the fabric, sometimes getting skirts caught, sometimes getting hair caught, sometimes hands or legs, working for hours and hours, never resting, breathing deadly dust—robbed of their childhoods, robbed of their dreams, and all for a measly TWO CENTS AN HOUR, while outside the birds sang and the blue sky shone.

I saw the gray line of children dressed in rags, heading home in the dreary dark of evening. I saw them collapse on their pallets of straw, too tired even to eat—

just to be forced back to work by the factory whistle at five a.m.

I saw burly foremen throwing the tots in through the factory doors when they were late, paddling them when they didn't work fast enough.

I saw their gnarled little hands, which looked like the hands of someone who'd been working eighty years. I saw their stooped backs and their missing fingers. CHILDREN!

I saw parents, too, standing side by side with their kids. It wasn't that they didn't love their darling babies. It was just that they were paid *so little* by the factory owners that their children HAD TO work—or *starve.*

Well, once you have seen cruelty, truly *seen* it, you can't just walk away. If you can't stop it, you've got to make sure *other people see it.* And that is what I did.

I called the newspapers.

Course, the newspapers were **owned** by rich folks who were buddies with the rich folks who owned the mills. And so they weren't about to print any stories that made the mill owners look as EVIL and GREEDY as they really were.

Money is a powerful thing. But there is power in the people. There is POWER in the UNION—the union of workers marching side by side, demanding better lives.

What—you never heard of a union? It's like a club for workers. And sometimes the workers in a union walk away from their jobs to protest unfair treatment. That's called a strike.

Well, boys and girls, I had an idea for a strike that those newsmen would **have** to write about in their stinking papers. . . .

"LISTEN TO MOTHER," I roared at a union meeting, "AND LET ME TAKE YOUR KIDS ON A **MARCH** THAT THE WORLD WILL **NEVER FORGET:** A PROTEST MARCH FROM PHILADELPHIA . . . TO NEW YORK CITY! IT'S TIME FOR FOLKS **TO SEE** HOW THE RICH GET RICHER ON THE BLOOD AND SWEAT OF THESE POOR LITTLE CHILDREN'S BACKS." People cheered and hollered—oh yes, I'd gotten them RILED UP.

A march it would be! Some parents packed their bags to join us. Others kissed their kids goodbye.

And on July 7, 1903, one hundred boys and girls set out, armed only with knapsacks containing a knife and fork, a tin cup and plate, and placards and banners that said WE WANT TIME TO PLAY and WE WANT TO GO TO SCHOOL.

At the front were three kids dressed like soldiers from the American Revolution. Why? Because just as the first Americans fought for their freedom, my little revolutionaries were a-fightin' for *their* freedom.

Flashbulbs flashed, and before you could say "Piscataway," we'd gotten our pictures in all the local papers.

"Where are you going?" asked a newsman.

"We're going to see the president!" I told him—and all the kids let out a whoop! This was my new plan: Why stop at New York? Why not march to the fancy-schmancy Long Island summer home of President Theodore Roosevelt himself?

So onward we marched. And what a sight we must've been: a bunch of scraggly ragamuffins with backpacks, out on the open road, led by a crazy old lady. Folks would stand and stare as we passed. Some would cheer us on. Some gave us food.

Sometimes train conductors would let us ride for free—just so
the kids could rest their poor little feet for a spell.

Sometimes we slept in people's barns.

Sometimes we camped out underneath the stars. This was the most fun the little tykes had ever had!

Mornings, we'd bathe in streams and rivers—the first time the kids had ever been swimming. It makes me weep to think of them.

But what they needed wasn't tears. And so in every town, I pulled out my stand, stepped right up on it, and proceeded to holler:

"JUST LOOK AT THIS LITTLE CHAP. HE'S STOOPED OVER LIKE AN OLD MAN FROM CARRYING BUNDLES OF YARN THAT WEIGH SEVENTY-FIVE POUNDS. HE GETS THREE DOLLARS A WEEK AND WORKS IN A CARPET FACTORY TEN HOURS A DAY WHILE THE CHILDREN OF THE RICH ARE GETTING THEIR HIGHER EDUCATION."

And when I got done talkin', some of the kids would put on a play. Dressed up like rich folks and factory owners, they'd prance about and have the crowd in stitches.

Then they'd pass the American flag around like a hat so people could throw in nickels and dimes—a lot of money for someone dirt-poor.

It took us fourteen days to march **a hundred miles** in the hot summer sun—sweat pouring off us, soaking our clothes. For fourteen days, we put on shows, in the towns of Bristol, Morrisville, Trenton, Princeton, New Brunswick, Metuchen, Rahway, Elizabeth, Jersey City, Hoboken. . . . For fourteen nights, we swatted mosquitoes. A lot of the kids couldn't take it—they headed back home.

By the time we crossed the Hudson River on a ferry bound for New York City, there were only thirty-seven kids left—and a few tired grown-ups.

That didn't matter. Our crusade had MADE IT. But we weren't DONE—
not hardly. And after we marched up Fourth Avenue by torchlight, the parade
route lined with six hundred cops, we just kept on marching . . .

. . . till we reached Coney Island, with its seaside amusement parks. My factory kids had never seen such a place—the Ferris wheel, the roller coaster, the big blue ocean. All they'd ever known was work. At last—a day of play!

But at day's end, it was time for a show.

I had the kids get inside some empty cages and pretend to be animals—so folks could see how these children were treated: **locked up.** And as they clung to the bars, I shouted loud above the ocean waves:

"AFTER A LONG AND WEARY MARCH, WE ARE ON OUR WAY TO SEE **PRESIDENT ROOSEVELT**. . . . WE WANT HIM TO HEAR THE WAIL OF THE CHILDREN WHO NEVER HAVE A CHANCE TO GO TO SCHOOL, BUT WORK FROM TEN TO ELEVEN HOURS A DAY IN THE TEXTILE MILLS . . . WEAVING THE CARPETS THAT HE AND YOU WALK ON, AND THE CURTAINS AND CLOTHES OF THE PEOPLE."

We DID want the president to hear us—but I had promised the parents of those kids to have them back home in ten days, and we'd already been on the road for twenty! So I sent most of my little troops home. What was left was just a motley crew— three boys, me, and a couple of men—sneakin' through the woods of Long Island.

By the time we got to the president's mansion, boy, were we tired and dirty. But we'd come this far. Surely he'd agree to see us: We were **Americans**. We were **humans**.

We stood at the gates—and were told that the president was "out." We were told we should write him a letter. We were told, in so many words, to get lost.

So this was how my *glorious* march was to end? With three tired children, sobbing because they knew they had to go back to the factory?

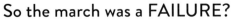

So the march was a FAILURE?

HECK, NO! What we did that summer changed the world. The Children's Crusade shined a great big SPOTLIGHT on child labor. Decent, good-hearted people finally SAW these kids who worked in factories. And that got people THINKING . . . which finally got them **DEMANDING** laws against child labor:

—**No child under the age of eighteen may work a dangerous job.**

—**No child under the age of sixteen may work during school hours.**

—**No child under the age of fourteen may work after school hours.**

And these laws helped get children where they belonged—out of FACTORIES, and into CLASSROOMS. It took nearly forty years for America to pass these laws, but as they say, *the wheels of justice grind slowly.* And sometimes you need a strong MOTHER to set them in motion.

And even when I'm dead and gone, I will be with you, my children—in the laws that protect you from working in factories. I will abide wherever there's a fight against wrong. I will abide—*in every fist that's raised against injustice.*

Author's Note

The woman the world knows as Mother Jones was born Mary Harris in County Cork, Ireland, on August 1, 1837, and immigrated with her family to Canada as a teenager. No stranger to hardship, she survived the Irish Potato Famine, the yellow fever epidemic of 1867 (to which she lost her husband, George Jones, and their four children), and the Great Chicago Fire of 1871 (to which she lost her home and dressmaking business). Around 1880, she got involved with the labor unions that were springing up all over America. By age sixty, she had gained such a beloved reputation with workers that she earned the nickname Mother. She was known forever after as Mother Jones, the most dynamic figure in American labor history.

She slept on the cold floors of workers' cabins, sometimes worked in the mills herself, and often got thrown in jail. Wherever workers were being mistreated—steel mills, cotton mills, coal mines, you name it—Mother Jones would step in. She encouraged them to organize unions, go on strike, and *stay* on strike. And if they were shot at by company guards, she encouraged them to defend themselves. However, she claimed to prefer "drama" to violence, and she understood the visual power of a little old lady publicly bellowing words of righteous outrage at injustice. For this reason, politicians called her the grandmother of all agitators and the most dangerous woman in America. Perhaps her greatest achievement was drawing attention to the horrors of child labor, especially with her Children's Crusade, the topic of this book. She died on November 30, 1930.

In her own way, Mother Jones is as important as Abraham Lincoln and Martin Luther King Jr. By law, American children now must go to school and are barred from working in factories—thanks in large part to Mother Jones. There are still countries where children work in factories, some of which produce American goods. Worldwide, there are 215 million child workers. And even here and now in America, there are adults who want to reverse child labor laws. We need Mother Jones.

Mother Jones with a group of girl strikers, 1903.

Mother Jones, 1910.

Mother Jones begins her "Children's Crusade" walk from Philadelphia to Oyster Bay, New York, to publicize working conditions of children in textile mills, 1903.

Mother Jones attends hearings of the federal Commission on Industrial Relations in New York City Hall, 1915.

Bibliography

Cohen, Adam. "Dirty Work: The Creeping Rollback of Child-Labor Laws." *Time*, June 6, 2011.

Foner, Philip S., ed. *Mother Jones Speaks: Speeches and Writings of a Working-Class Fighter.* New York: Pathfinder Press, 1983.

Freedman, Russell. *Kids at Work: Lewis Hine and the Crusade Against Child Labor.* New York: Clarion Books, 1994.

Gorn, Elliott J. *Mother Jones: The Most Dangerous Woman in America.* New York: Hill and Wang, 2002.

"Hear 'Mother' Jones Talk." *The New York Times*, July 25, 1903.

Jones, Mary Harris. *Autobiography of Mother Jones.* Mineola, NY: Dover Publications, 2012.

"List of Goods Produced by Child Labor or Forced Labor." Washington, D.C.: U.S. Department of Labor, 2012.

McCarthy, Ryan. "13 Products Most Likely to Be Made by Child or Forced Labor." *Huffington Post*, May 25, 2011.

"'Mother' Jones at Passaic." *The New York Times*, July 21, 1903.

"'Mother' Jones's Army Parades." *The Washington Post*, July 24, 1903.

Niell, Charles Patrick. "Report on Conditions of Women and Child Wage-Earners in the United States." Washington, D.C.: U.S. Bureau of Labor Statistics, 1910.

"Sit down and read. Educate yourself for the coming conflicts."

"You must stand for free speech in the streets."

"I am not unaware that leaders betray, and sell out, and play false."

"And who is responsible for this appalling child slavery? Everyone!"

"The future is in labor's strong, rough hands."

"No matter what your fight, don't be ladylike!"

"Not all the coal that is dug warms the world."

"My address is like my shoes: it travels with me.... I abide where there is a fight against wrong."